# Dispatch From the Far Land

## NEW POEMS

*June Sidran Mandelkern*

Dispatch From the Far Land

June Sidran Mandelkern
jsmandelkern@gmail.com

Book design by Kathy Strauss, ImageWerks
kathy@imagewerks.net

Printed in the United States of America, 2023

Cover Photograph:
*Farmington River Trail, Burlington, CT, 2023*
All photographs by Mervyn Strauss
sequin2@comcast.net

# *Acknowledgments*

Many thanks:

to my friend Adlyn Loewenthal, whose care and compassion jump-started this book, and followed it to it's conclusion;

to Kathy Strauss, beloved daughter of my partner and consummate artist, who put it together and made it happen;

to the memory of my deceased husband Robert Mandelkern, who helped me find the path I walk today;

to my sister Sonya Greenfield, friend and companion from the beginning, whose strength and courage is a beacon of light, and to the memory of our sister, Miriam Sidran, who is with us always;

to my friends in poetry, Marcia Lewis, librarian who founded the Faxon Poets and showed me the way, and Sharon Cormier who shares with me her creative spirit and encourages mine;

to my sons Nicolas, Michael and Peter/Owa Mandelkern and their devoted partners and spouse Susan Forrest, Myrna Rasmussen and K.C. Gesin, who sustain and support me always;

and to my amazing grandchildren Talya, Carmi, Ronit, Neal and Nora Mandelkern who light up my world and carry me into the future.

*For Merv Strauss, companion, friend and partner, who shares with me the joys and challenges of our later years.*

# Contents

# I
# Generations

*Kenya – 2007*

# Memorial Candle

I light the memorial candle for my mother
on the anniversary of her death.

My sons, her grandsons, do not recall the date,
they were young and death had little meaning for them,
nor do their sons and daughters, her great grandchildren,
not even the one named for her,
who carry her into the future but never knew her.

I hold the tiny vessel in my hand.
The flame glows pure and sweet, lighting
my kitchen wall. So did the ancient gift of fire
illuminate the huge expanse of darkness
for our earliest ancestors, to penetrate
the mysteries of life and love.

This gift of light is all that I can give her now.
As long as I remember her, she lives.

One day will someone light a candle for me?
Will it matter to the universe
or to me?

# The Young Women

The young women, I love to see them
clutching books tightly in their arms
or pushing strollers to the library
and the shops on Main Street,

Legs sturdy or slim
brightly encased in patterned tights,
long sweaters hanging loosely
according to the fashion of the day,
with sneakers or practical shoes
and jackets snugly fastened
against the winter chill.

American to the core,
they know the world awaits
the sound of their voices
and the firm tread of their heels
in the corridors of power.

We, my friends and I,
their mothers, aunts and grandmothers
who have walked the paths they walk today,
we spread our canopy of love
beneath their wings
and, awestruck, watch them as they fly.

# Old Women in
# the Locker Room

Old women in the locker room
undress for the water aerobics class
at the local community center,
push their fleshy breasts into too-small cups
of faded swimsuits, and swollen feet
into bright colored sandals.
Eager as girls, they head for the pool
chatting in several languages, holding off
the ravages of time one more day.

Husbands long gone,
sustained by their children,
skin deeply wrinkled and bodies sagging
from years of toil and stress,
their unfailing courage astounds me.

No reporters come to interview them,
no medals are awarded to them,
no platform is theirs on which to speak.
Unnoticed and invisible they survive
to return day after day,
the brave old women in the locker room
at the local community center.

# For Cantor Siskin

Giant heart in a pixie body
dancing on air with arms
outstretched to embrace the world,
voice endowed by angels
with humor to lighten sadness and pain,
for almost two decades you have been
our spiritual mentor, our loving guide
in song and prayer of Jewish life.

Teacher and friend to young and old,
weddings and funerals, weekly worship,
children's school and choir practice,
b'nai mitzvah and Purim spiel,
holiday services and senior group,
you have inspired us to sing
in praise of Torah and all humankind.

Pamela, as the tide of life now turns
to carry you to other pastures,
we who have been blessed
with your radiant presence
give you our blessings now:

May the journey ahead be fruitful
for you and your loving spouse,
may the winds be fair at your back,
may you find safe haven in a peaceful place,
may health and joy be your portion
and may the bottomless well
of your faith and lovingkindness
sustain you in the years to come.

# Generational Joy

There is no greater joy than a phone call
from an adult grandchild who says
she is thinking of you.

She is a third year medical student
at the University of Pittsburgh Medical Center.
She tells me she is exhausted
but the lilt in her voice belies her words.
Her cat, brought from home, is sad
because she has so little time to play with him.
In the midst of clinical rotations
she must choose her professional path.
She is thinking of hospital work with
children and adults, perhaps in cardiology.

She tells me about her time in the trauma unit
treating gunshot and stabbing injuries.
I see her clearly, five feet tall,
unruly curls tucked firmly under her cap,
dressing wounds, absorbed
in the miraculous world of healing.

When she was five she said to me,
You love me the best because I was the first.
If there is a kernel of truth in these words
I dare not say.  She is my heart, my spirit,
my bridge to the future.

I hunger for some words of medical wisdom
from the fledgling physician.
She only says, take care of yourself.
She will be home for the holidays.
My cup runneth over.

# For Talya

*On your graduation from medical school,*
*as you enter the professional world of medicine:*

My first-born grandchild,
first child of my first-born son,
you hold a special place in my heart.

As a girl-child you played
not with baby dolls and tea sets,
but with communities of stuffed animals
and other more fanciful ones
you created from plastic rods and blocks.
We told you there were no limits
to what you could become,
and happily you believed us.

Family can provide the uplift for your flight
and a parachute to catch you if you fall:

But now, your great achievement,
born of your own hard work, dedication, and resolve,
belongs to you alone.

# II
# European Travel

*Florence, Italy – 2018*

# Courtyard in Florence

The view from my hotel room
overlooks the roofs of Florence,
corrugated rows of round red tiles
dotted with skylights, antennas
stark against the sky. Across the courtyard
the back wall of the building opposite
shows tall glass doors, curtained or shuttered,
bordered by narrow balconies festooned
with plants. Small windows open outward
ornamented with clothes lines stretched between.

In the apartment across the way
a woman appears at her window
to hang her wash. Absorbed in her task
she pulls the lines closer, securing the clothes
with pins: the universal task of women
to conquer dirt and disorder. Blue jeans
and underwear, sheets and towels,
table cloths and baby shirts flap loosely
in the soft breeze. I worry that
she may lose her balance
leaning out to reach for them!

On the streets below narrow sidewalks
worn with the tread of centuries
are crowded with pedestrians
interwoven with bicycles and motor vehicles.
Occasional ambulance sirens
punctuate the air, noises of the city
audible in my perch.

To the woman of the courtyard I silently speak:
I greet you as a traveler from a distant world
across the cultures that separate us.
I admire your industry and control
as much as I am privileged to share it.
For this small glimpse of your life
I thank you. Woman to woman,
I wish you well. Ciao!

# When in Rome

Don't wait for the 115 bus, our guide says,
and the 872 Is not too great either.
Our guide is a transplanted Texan living
with his American father and Italian mother
in Rome. Don't wait for the 115, he says,
only partly in jest, it will never come.

The 115 is one of only two buses
to the children's hospital, and the company
has not bought any new ones in years, he says.
If you wait at the bus stop you will wait…and wait…

Sure enough, in the square
in front of the statue of Garibaldi high atop his horse
with the bas-relief on the base of Romulus and Remus
nursing at the she-wolf, we come across
a broken-down 115 bus waiting to be towed away.

From the top of the hill we take photos
of the rooftops of Rome with the rounded
Pantheon dome in the direction of our hotel.
Our guide identifies the Jewish synagogue and
various churches out to St. Peter's Basilica
in the distance. The weather is glorious in October,
the crowds less dense than in summer.

In two weeks we have become quite Italian,
comfortably handling our euros, finishing dinner
at ten PM, choosing wines and desserts carefully
with the genial support of voluble waiters,
walking narrow cobble-stoned streets dodging autos
and cycles weaving through, miraculously hitting no one.

Suddenly as if a switch is pulled our time is up:
home beckons, efficient and practical. If ever
we return to Rome we will remember:
Don't wait for the 115 bus, it will never come.

# Interlude in Madrid

I sit on a bench on a sandy path
of the Royal Botanic Gardens in the heart of Madrid.
It is late afternoon on my last day in Spain.
Outside the iron gate homegoing traffic
on the Calle de Prado joins the background noise.
Here welcome silence reigns.

The park, laid out in geometric pattern
of circles, squares and triangles
is spare, not lush in the tradition
of more humid climes. The stone-robed statue
of King Carlos III, creator of the gardens,
barely shields me from the still-warm sun.
Oversized bees hover on white flowers
under the pale unbroken canopy of sky.
An occasional visitor strolls by
dressed casually in these early days of fall.

Protected from the loud civic demonstrations
parading on the streets all day
I spend my last few hours inhaling the peace
that humans are capable of producing
in the center of chaos. Here on this sturdy bench
far from home, part of the living fabric
of this vibrant city, my spirit is released.

I will not soon return to this quiet place.
Tomorrow a giant bird will carry me back
to the pulsating rhythm of my own reality.
But I have had these calming moments
to renew my belief in humankind
and fortify me to resume my journey
through life in the days ahead.

# III
# *Playful Poems*

*Joker Playing Card – 2023*

# Adam was Late

Picture Eve waiting in the garden
dreaming of her lover,
longing for his touch,

strong arms to hold her fast,
sweet words of love
to promise everlasting bliss...

What if Adam had not tarried,
had not missed his cue?
What if he were there in the garden
to clasp her in his warm young arms,
cover her lips with kisses,
claim her full attention
not to be distracted?

Picture Eve arriving at the garden
to find her lover impatiently waiting
to seize her in his strong young arms,
closing her mouth with kisses...

Could they—could we—have lived
in innocence forever?

Oh brave young world,
did our future hinge on invention
of a watch?

# For Emily Dickinson

Today I wrote a poem,
Exuberant I get.
Whether it is any good
I cannot tell just yet.

Pleasure is in the doing,
Vindication of my soul.
Today I wrote a poem,
Proof tomorrow still is whole.

# IV
## New Love

*The Kiss – Auguste Rodin*
*Paris, France – 2016*

# Hand in Hand

The sight of an older couple
walking hand in hand
fills my heart with joy.

Thus it is we walk together,
you and I,
your tall body sheltering my smaller one
as I slip my hand in yours.

Your large palm and supple fingers
close over mine, enfolding them
In warmth and safety.
We move without conscious volition
In absolute peace and trust.

If our hands were a sentient being
it would breathe a long exhalation
of relief and comfort, saying:

    this is our destination,
    this is where we belong,
    this is our home in the spheres,

as earth and sky hold
their proper place In the cosmos
and we walk together
hand in hand
one more day.

# Love Song

Romantic love after the age of ninety
would seem to be a non-sequitur.

Body parts sag, unwrinkled skin
and waistlines are photos in an album.
In the midst of passion leg cramps appear,
quiet time ends in stiffness and backache.
Improvisation is required, powered by memory.
Yet when he calls me beautiful, I am.

Oh, the joy, improbability of it all,
the sense of special gladness,
gifts of love improvidently given.
We are alone in an alternate universe,
minds and bodies intertwined.

We wonder, does it show? I slip my hand in his,
the need to connect overwhelming.
There is some sense of safety too, I must not trip
on pavement or stairs.  One fall could end it all.

The window of opportunity is narrow,
the road ahead mined: the mantra,
live for today, feel the moment,
never so poignantly true. We marvel
at resilience of the human spirit,
this wondrous gift of time,
this tardy burst of glory,
this lyrical coda to the symphony of life.

"Ah, love, let us be true to one another!"
These are all the words I know,
or need to know, for now.

# Tanka 1-2-3

1
in old age our love
came unbidden from the stars
tardy burst of joy
lyrical coda added
to the symphony of life

2
in our sunset years
unexpected love appeared
melodies of hope
join in the swelling chorus
of our last great song of life

3
in fullness of age
love flew in on wings of joy
flowers of life spread
beauty one more day before
they fade and die forever

# V
# *Nonagenarian Musings*

*Rocking Chairs – 2023*

# Faces in the Mirror

Two strange old people
dwell in our bathroom:
who they might be
we do not know.
Unfamiliar faces
stare from the mirror.

Hair graying to white,
skin wrinkled and blemished,
unfocused glances peer at us.
We turn away in disbelief
and switch off the light.

Who gave them permission
to occupy our space?
Certainly not he nor I.
We are fair with strong limbs,
agile bodies and smooth skin,
active minds roaming free.
From which sad fantasy
have they been created?

We go about our work,
pursue our daily lives,
meet with our friends,
pretend we do not see.
A moment's inattention
could summon them,
smiling and real,
from the other side of the glass.

# Justice Ginsburg and Me

Who am I, today?
In appearance, an old woman with gray hair
wearing beige capri pants in deference
to the last days of summer just before
the solstice that ushers in the fall.
My long-sleeved shirt has purple,
black and aqua flowers on a white background,
and I wear a cotton cardigan sweater
to ward off the autumn chill.

I am somewhat fashionable in a contemporary way,
not your typical old lady, if such a one exists today.
Another old woman, Justice Ruth Bader Ginsberg,
died a few days ago. Nine years my junior,
she was born to Jewish parents in Brooklyn,
as was I. She graduated from my high school,
James Madison, and was reportedly a good student,
as was I, although I did not go to law school
and end up on the Supreme Court.
She had two children and I had three,
both of us with satisfactory long-term marriages
and no inclination for cooking, according
to the stories told about her.

Her legacy is strong and powerful,
legal advocate for women everywhere.
The country and the world are in mourning.
Her body rested in state in the national capital,
the first woman to be given that honor.
Her death precipitated a national crisis,
to fill her liberal vacancy on the Court:
which mine of course, when it comes, will not.

I hope I will fade from life quietly
as the waters gently close over my head.
My children will mourn, and my grandchildren.
My legacy will be my poems, and with Justice Ginsberg,
my dementia-free longevity,
my passion for exercise,
my love for justice and family
and a life well-spent In caring.

# Word Magic

I found a lovely poem today.
It appeared on my mobile phone
In the obituary of a local poet
who died too soon at 62,
about the age of my sons.
Truly I was not expecting it.

It does happen occasionally
that by chance some perfect lines,
new to me or old,
touch my heart.  At such a time
I am moved beyond thought.

Now I am flooded with relief
that the beauty of the word
still has the power to reach
the inner recess of my mind,
awaken the still small voice of self
buried beneath everyday indignities
of the aging human life.

# Quiet Peace of August

The trees stand calm and still today, no branch stirs.
Chipmunks, birds and squirrels,
the rabbit who delights my sense of childishness,
all gone to rest.  One errant leaf
drifts softly down to lie upon the grass.

The quiet peace of August is here again,
the lush blue-green of late summer foliage
imprinted on the sky
teases us with knowledge
of the season to come.

In 2020, year of the great pandemic plague,
the human population of earth,
weary and anxious,
seeks respite from misery and pain.
Sea levels rise, monster storms
gather strength from warming oceans,
tsunamis threaten vulnerable coasts,
war and unrest, hunger and death are rampant.
True to our tribal heritage we turn
one against the other, seeking advantage
in a shifting world.

May the quiet peace of August fill our hearts
with sustenance and hope
to guide us
through the long hard winter ahead.

# Silent Witness

The large round shrub seen through my window
at the edge of the yard is aflame with autumn color.
Sunlight gleams on bright orange foliage
reflected through clear yellow on taller trees
and the deep tone of evergreens beyond.
The grass, still green, is littered with fallen leaves
muted in tan and gold.  In the still air no errant breeze
stirs, the only movement the rippling caused
by unseen squirrels scampering up the trunks.

The earth waits, this moment etched in time.
I, the silent witness, wait too.
My heart is with the squirrels, warm blooded,
gathering their winter sustenance,
preparing for an unknown future.
A few dry leaves drift slowly down.
why those and none other?
When will it be my turn?

In the tenth decade of my life,
acknowledging no deity
to thank for all this splendor,
my gratitude goes to the providence
that has granted me this perfect favor
one more time.

# In One More Year...

I have said it before:  I was born in 1924,
in one more year I will be 100.
One hundred times the earth will have journeyed
around the sun since my mother held me to her breast.

Like Walt, I celebrate myself.
I can walk upright, put one suitably shod foot
before the other without assistance.
My mind, somewhat supple, is still able to dream.

I can unlock the door of my old Toyota
bought twenty years ago in another town,
another state, another time, and drive myself
to get my hair cut and my nails polished,
marveling at the clear blue of the sky
with the imprint of trees green in outline upon it.
I care enough about my world
to notice the lawn signs, Black Lives Matter,
and the rainbow flags waving in the breeze.

I can enjoy a tennis tournament on television,
the thrill of lithe young bodies striking the balls
with precision and strength, recalling
my active young husband on a long ago
Saturday morning in sneakers and shorts
heading toward the town courts, racket in hand,
with the children and myself safely at home.

My life is a poem in progress waiting
for the final lines to tie it all together
and give substance to the words written before.
I have said it before: I was born in 1924
and in one more year...

# 1924

My birthday has arrived.
I was born in 1924. I always thought
It was a good year to be born,
unless you were a Jewish girl growing up
in Germany or Poland or even France
or almost any place in Europe.

Thanks to enterprising ancestors
I am a citizen of the United States
not accessible to Nazi genocide:
a Yankee, one of the eastern elite
so vilified in the heartland.

Returning to the subject at hand,
my birthday: momentous or portentous,
who knows?  I feel no difference from yesterday,
no premonition of imminent disaster.

I look forward to a peaceful future
of friendship and sun, flowers rioting
on the back porch, lettuce and herbs
ready to be picked for dinner,
tomatoes ripening in the garden,
poems waiting to be written
and people to be loved.

Was 1924 a good year to be born?
We'll wait and see.

# About the Author

June Sidran Mandelkern was
born in 1924 in Brooklyn, N.Y.
She attended local schools,
including two years at Brooklyn
College. In 1968 she earned a
BA degree at Hunter College of
City University of New York,
and in 1996 an MS degree in
Geoscience at Montclair State
University in New Jersey. Her
husband of sixty years, Robert
Mandelkern, a World War II veteran, died in 2013. She has
three sons and five grandchildren.

June began writing poetry seriously after moving to Connecticut
in 2001. She has published two books of poems: *Reflections,*
Tall Trees Press, 2009; and *To the Far Country,* published by
Amazon.com., 2016. Both books are available on loan from
the Noah Webster Library of West Hartford, CT. She is proud
to be a founding member of the Faxon Poets of West Hartford
and to have participated in all of their published anthologies,
*Perspectives I-XIII,* 2006–2019, in which some of these poems
have appeared. She lives in West Hartford with her partner, also
a World War II veteran, Mervyn Strauss.

jsmandelkern@gmail.com

Made in the USA
Middletown, DE
03 September 2023